Unnamed Poetry

Murat Tali

2024

Contents

Life's Poetry

From experiences you can't name
Can a poem be nameless?
If hundreds come together,
To form a book of words,
What name shall we call

From experiences you can't name
While you are the creditor the most,
Why does everyone claim ownership of you life?

If poetry is nothing more than a poet's madness,
Then why do people think?

Love, longing, affection, death, hope,
Are told solely by poets and in poems?

If two sentences and ten words make a poem,
Why don't those vast experiences
Not a single person does?

Why can't we live like a poem
And
We can't be like in poetry our lives?

By delegating poems to poets
Is it not because we try to live
Our suffering

Myself

On one side is anarchy,
On the other, tranquillity – whatever exists,
All is MYSELF.

One side is unhappiness and pain,
The other side, pure happiness,
Whatever pertains to identity,
All is MYSELF.

Hell comes into existence,
Grows with the sum of sins,
Heaven exists,
Nourished by virtues, its gates open,
The product that emerges has a single name,
MYSELF.

Sometimes you rebel against existence,
Other times you bless everything that happens.
You try to solve all these events by seeking a culprit,
Someone talks about Oneness, a culprit is found,
Once again, MYSELF.

Someone creates religion,
Someone models gods,
Someone gives them names,
If you believe in all of them,
What will be lost,
Once again, MYSELF.

Chaos descends, the world crumbles,
Thieves take their lead and depart,

Killers multiply,
Murders are committed,
Rapes increase,
Aberrations occur,
A voice speaks and says,
"Everything is a reflection of something, and what you see is your reflection,"
The pumpkin bursts open again,
Responsibility is scattered in the public square,
The sole culprit is found;
Once again, MYSELF.

At times,
You get lost in the material world,
At times, you seek the path in the spiritual realm,
With every action done and action taken, you search for a solution,
What you need to find when you search,
Once again, MYSELF.

In a life so full of MYSELF,
Isn't there even a hint
Of YOUR fault or contribution?
Do they not ask the person?

And if you ask, they say, "Do not create duality..."
Everything is the manifestation and experience of ONENESS,
You remain as the perpetrator of all your crimes in the public square;
Who is the culprit?
Once again, MYSELF...

Away with it.

Untimely breakups

We live our separations according to custom.
In our pockets, the seal of Sultan Süleyman,
On our backs, the eyes of David.
Saying, "The below is the same as the above,"
We sacrifice all our loves
To a single message.

When Jesus was crucified,
He cried out in the darkness
The cry of the surrender of love.
His disciples,
On the day of the solstice of separation,
Searching for the beloved,
God was once again addicted to solitude.

Because he was owed by Nimrod,
Abraham had brought forth spring from fire.
For his love of Zeliha,
Hagar cried out for Abraham.
"What kind of destruction is this?"
Your god fights with the love that fell into my womb,
And the desert is devastated.

In the redness of the last drop of blood that fell to the sand,
In the tears of Ishmael, who was born,
All lovers whose prayers are to be reunited
Have burned and turned to ashes in the fire of separation
In this world.

That is why,

Every lover who is afraid of fire
Makes his heart experience separations
Without falling into the fire.

Hurt

It hurt, oh master, it hurt so much,
The pain goes so deep that even saying "it didn't hurt"
Goes deeper than the depths of pain
In the human heart.

When you say "it didn't hurt,"
The tears that well up in your eyes
Are the greatest proof of the timidity,
The cowardice,
The escape from yourself
That lie hidden within those tears.

It hurt, oh master,
It hurt so much,
The important thing is to accept that pain
And to transform it into love
And to release it from the heart.

Otherwise, this pain will always hurt the heart.

It hurt, oh master,
It hurt so much it made me bleed
And took my tears from my lungs
And delivered them to a raging pain
By hurting me.
You have to smile in defiance
In defiance of everything that hurts
and hurts.

What was Truth?

What was Love?
What was Breath?
What was Man?
What was Faith?
What was Death?
……what happened to life?

Beloved

"Perchance, love they called it,
was but a spark of fire that resided solely in thine heart...

And the beloved they spoke of,
was naught but a flint struck by that spark...
Thine affliction was to burn, its duty to ignite.

Given thou art engulfed in flames,
now neither beloved nor spark is needed...
Already thou art ash, transformed into ember,
beyond the moment,
what need for the beloved?

Mystery

Since light does not hide us
We hide our dreams in the darkness,
Our love that we keep inside
So that it will not be revealed.

Desist not from loving, child

Should Azrael claim thy soul,
If the bridge of Sırat measures thy life,
If fire outweighs on the scale,
Then cease not from love, O child.

For each fire,
Burns only as much as a spark of love
Consumes thy soul at most,
And thou, too,
Shalt declare, "I have lived this life."

Bloodshot

My eyes are bloodshot,
A weariness of my sleepless nights doth dwell,
A heavy, medieval stench doth waft over me,
A splash of mud, I am distant from all paths,
As I cover my nakedness in mud,
I return to the statues found in ancient ruins,
The brush bristles touch my broken arms and wings,
I grieve despite the serenity of the centuries,
Without losing anything from my time.

My Dreams

'Twixt my nails, my ensnared dreams have descended,
I have built circuses in the sky,
To delight the spoiled child within me,

I take smiling pictures,
Leaning against the moon's back.
I sway my feet in the sea,
My hair accompanies comets.

In my eyes, desert winds where my lashes have nestled.
My name is the sibling narrative of the universe,
My skin, castles of sand.

Africa

Today,
from a land I've never known,
I will call out to you, my darling,
Perhaps from Africa.

From my black skin,
I will gaze at you with smiling eyes,
With the whiteness of my palms,
I will hold your white neck,
I will scatter the hopes I have gathered from you
Among the green oases,

I will run like a gazelle clinging to life,
In front of the lions,
And I will embrace you like a lion.

I will build my nest on the steep slopes of the mountains,
We will fly with the eagles over the savannas of Africa,
The Nile will flow from our lips,
Pharaohs will reign,
From the happiness that falls from our paws,

The Red Sea will be inspired by Moses,
The Torah will open its door,
The oases will speak of you.

Our name will be Africa,
Our color will be black,
A white daisy will sprout in our palms,

Filling your heart with the inspiration of the sun-kissed skin,
Africa
shall surrender to a yellow dream,
Liberated from the burning desert climates,
The sandstorms,
The arid lands.

Our name will be Africa, my darling,
The land of a black love,
Wrapped in red dreams.

Loneliness

At times,
I ponder the lossed of my syllables.
Neither in my left pocket remain the words,
Nor in my right pocket,

I fall into a peculiar wave,
Waves sway me in their palms,

My mind becomes entangled,
I descend into syllables.
I ignite a light,
Dancing on the water's surface,

named it sea sparkle
Sharing your solitude with myself.

I am left alone,
And a tiny drop on my skin,
With the residue of the ocean's presence,
I name it a "tear"
Gracefully flowing
From myself
To myself.

The Wayfarers

Those who have departed, those who have arrived, those who remain,
Observers and beholders, listeners,
And those who have never been.
Where everyone is a wayfarer.

Some sing a duet
With their loneliness hidden behind the mists.
Some lose themselves
In the crowd that has set out on the road.

On the roads,
There are footprints
That seem to lead from the past to the future,
But in reality,
They are stealing moments from the future
To save the day.

If a forest were to blaze,
in its embers, my dreams fry like fish.

The trees are uprooted,
With their longings laden on their branches,
A yellow daisy falls into my eyes,
With its secrets in its cage,
My feet
Tread the snowy mountains.

Do not stop like that,
Holding your heart in your hands
As if you carry the world on your head.

Be aware of the sun above you,
Child,
Even in your darkness,
With your night-black hair,
You carry the day that has been taken from life
On your life.

In paintings,
It is a virtue to gaze into the distance,
As a human or as a dog,
Even if it is not where you are looking,
Happiness is surely there,
Where you see and touch.

So,
Who is aware of your searches?
You hide them in your basket
Like a bride's dowry.

Only a rose
Can warm my heart,
But
Everywhere is freezing with longing
And the scent of longing.

Colossal a folly

Oh, the weight that entwines my heart,
And the night's cloud, laden with sorrow,
Silently drifting,
Once again, a tempest stirs
In the remotest corner of my universe.
If you will rain, rain now,
Before the mists cover everything,

Perhaps the most challenging aspect of being human,
I believe, is carrying within one's heart
A love that's as heavy as a blacksmith's anvil.
To comprehend
The essence
And the lived experiences,

To some, it's love,
To others, a loss,
And to some, it may be
A colossal
Foolishness

The Man of No Character

He had words without character,
That bowed like italic letters
In the face of tyranny,
And his truth fed on human life.

It would enter the sanctuary and depart diminished,
Instead of surrendering itself,
It left behind its humanity every time.
Where he should have given up his soul.
He never grew,
But always thought himself a giant,
And he would throw love
To the senseless acts of
Unread prayers and
Unperformed sunnahs.

He never grew,
Until he entered the grave
Made of giant stones.
He died with the rights of others,
And voices rose,
"May God have mercy on those
You tried to take."
The sky above fell silent,
And waited for the arrival
Of the guardians of mercy at the door.

The Surrender

Ah, the clumsy surrender of tardiness,
Whenever I see you
At the window,
You always
Bring the same image
To my face,
That bittersweet
Face of your radiant
And shining smile,
And my orphaned dreams.

My surrender to time
Determines the size of the shroud
The size of my grave
Is measured by the sum of the unlived moments.

I had my bed dug vertically, not horizontally,
So that my face is always turned to the Kaaba.
In this way, the world turns around me,
Carrying my body in the middle.

The pieces that break off my body
Fill
The mouths of ants and worms.
My shroud is bleeding,
From the sins it has committed,
It wraps my bones even tighter.

My body
Is filled with pain.
That my eyes cannot see

And my skin cannot feel,
As the world turns.
But I
Deceived it,
Gave it my body and took my soul
From it.

My soul,
My soul,
A sweet child
Swinging in a swing,
The wind is working within me,
The clouds are enveloping.
The chaos of my mind that is shivering.
In spite of the pain of my body,
It is becoming even more loving.

My soul,
With its laughter,
In the sky,
One side of me is earth,
One side of me is sky now,
I am both in the heavens and on the earth,
With the light that is breathed into me.

The time of love's leftovers

In a distant city,
In a faraway street,
In the morning frost of a faraway city,
Love was born...

The garbage collectors saw it sometimes,
The gypsies who rummaged through the trash,
Some picked it up with their brooms,
Some threw it into their bags with their hands.

Time went by,
Love began to show itself in the afternoon,
This time, passersby saw it,
People on the crowded streets bumped into it,
With every bump, a piece of love was left behind,
and
It began to fade slowly.
love

The day turned into night,
Love transformed itself into neon lights,
It danced and laughed in the streets,
Then morning came,
Love collapsed tiredly at a street corner,

A garbage collector did pick it up with his broom,
He threw it into the back of the garbage truck,

And they separated love,
One worker tucked a piece into his pocket,
And a young garbage collector took another piece.

To give to his mother,

And his mother
Placed it in her display window,
As an old image that.

The Beggar of Love

Perhaps it should have never been,
That beloved draped in the fire called love,
Neither Adam would descend to this world,
Neither Nor would Eve have realized
The difference between birth and death.

If the creature called man had traveled In dry submission,
without hope.
He would not have lost his paradise,
Nor would he have been the
instrument of God's creation of hell.

Everything was for love,
Even the first death
Was for love.
In the fire of Cain and Abel,
All intentions were consumed.
All deaths and births
Were for love.
In the world, the exile of the soul,

God created man for love,
And he also immersed his own soul and essence
He immersed her in love.
If love is the other name of God,
At every moment man is with him,
In himself,
Otherwise life is already
A great hell...

The Poem of the Sea

Pablo Neruda said that a poem is never written in vain,
And the poem continues to be written into the void at every moment.
I looked inside and wondered, could a void and a wind cling to a poem and be poured out?
Here is a poem just for you, so read it to yourself...

I don't know which side of me is the river and which side is the sea.
My love is not enough for my body, even if it fills my soul.
The last moments of separation are being torn apart by the teeth of a rodent.
Slogans were shouted, "No death for us,"
And another me was dying in nothingness at every moment...

Bittersweet sorrows filled my lovemaking,
A drop of sweat falling on my beloved's chest was worth three pounds of joy.
Now the reunions
Were multiplying the struggles that had no extensions within it
And Dede Korkut was telling all his stories
To the unruly child within me.
My life was taking lives from a river,
My eyes were pouring out like the sea,
Scorching my longing lips with its salt...

The dreams sacrificed to love

Were becoming the offerings of a man who could not pray.
Just now,
Death was becoming the henna that spread on the palm of a Kurdish girl in the middle of the Euphrates and Tigris.
Who should love?
Who should die?
Children were growing up without knowing

Separation smelled of the blood that was smeared on the foreheads of children,
And the veil of the bride was coming to the bullets.
My love said to grow up every night while listening to the fairy tales of distant countries,
And my mother was still saluting the rising sun in the morning.
Her lamp smelled of kerosene, my grandfather would recite his sayings in case Khizr would knock on his door.

My love is strange,
Multiplying loves across the sea,
It comes and goes with the tides,
Like water, it falls and rises.

Love, An Anarchic Sentiment

LOVE, is an anarchic sentiment for the body,
And it incites rebellion in every cell of the mind.

LOVE, is immeasurable.
That's why it doesn't care how much debt you'll accumulate or it's how much you'll gain in the end.

LOVE, chooses to be irrational.
It knows that where reason enters, interrogations follow.

However, LOVE
Means surrendering to acceptance,
This is known, this is declared in all sacred texts.

And
LOVE takes its first action,
Occupies a heart,
Raises a banner and cries out into the night.
I LOVE YOU, MY BELOVED... SURRENDER TO MY HEART
And it burns the whole body
As if condemned to thirsty planets

The Last Gasp of the Human Spirit

The dream of man,
So crowded with words,
his life
Invaded by words,
and
Poetry is his last breath

That's why,
love and
revolution,
taking the poet as their shield,
takes refuge in poetry.

Love Born Beyond God

As history plucks the cartilage-like loves from my heart,
The birth of love without a body had been a test of four angels,
My soul had reached the joyous feast of Israfil's trumpet call,
Creation was meant to be known, but my creation story revolved around love.

Mikail, the guardian, became the spokesman for my boundless geographies,
Azrael cradled the embers of fires lit in temples thousands of years ago in his palm,
The laughter of God ignited fires in the fragrant gardens of heaven,
Billions of souls clothed themselves in bodies, and God forgot,
Some names,
Some blessings,
Some love was placed incomplete on the scales,
The excuse was clear,
You abandoned me for Love, O human,
But I, I had created you from myself to feel that love...

The human fell silent,
Taking Jesus down from the crucifix planted in the place called Hell,
She shed tears painted in red during an untimely desert storm,
Mortals do not smell of love, Beloved,
Let us take the stories about us from the Preserved Tablet and dip them in love,

Then, let us sit on the seventh floor of the world
Let us smile
At the children born of our love

Love Comes to the Soul

Fire ignites the soul,
Breath becomes intertwined,
The burning flesh becomes,
All that remains is the ego,
If you burn the ego,
Body becomes a cage for the ego.

O, who places worldly loves in your heart,
If you love with your ego,
You must set fire to the curtains of the heart,
If you love with your body
You must burn the veils of the heart.

Love should come from the essence,
neither ego
neither the body
Shouldn't be a slave
to your loves

Love, the White Shawl

Love is a white shawl,
Which becomes soiled with use.
It is washed to clean it,
But the more it is washed,
The more it fades.
As it fades, it tears,
And as it tears,
It loses its value.
As it loses its value,
It is cast aside,
And a new shawl is taken.

Love is a white shawl,
But I loved you in crimson.

genesis

The Creation of a Soul

In which body were you born, child?
To which love did you arrive too late?
At what age were you without a story?
From whom did life take your sins?
Do those who love you also keep your loved ones far away in life?
Did the loneliness of the last times emerge in its name?
Or did the silence of tomorrows clothe itself in the robe of desolation?
Your joys were so immense
Did their existence go unnoticed in blind bodies?
And life, believing that the branches it would hold onto were pruned for the return of spring,
Becomes the exile where wishes awaken at the time of the new moon under the full moon.

You know how they tell stories of things like meeting and parting,
They are tales and human dream stories.
A heap of tales without heroes but with names,
Perhaps the crumbs of yesterday's meal spilled from the writer's thoughts.
Like the ache of a child who has embraced his mother's longing in his heart.
Multiply your orphanhood in songs that smell of sorrow.

If your journey was written in ancient and modern times,
Reinscribe the yearning on walls with hieroglyphs.
Rebuild the Tower of Babel anew.
Bring down God Jehovah from His throne,
and express your grievances to Him.

Did you split me, from my tongue, my essence, myself, my humanity?
Was it to reach You?
All these events.

Then turn thy face to the North Star and make thy wish.
That thou mayest also write happy tales that will be read in the future.

The Fire of Zoroaster

Burn from the fire of Zoroaster, and set heaven aflame as well,
Burn, so that the entire universe may find balance at last,
For as long as humanity exists, hell grows the most,
Life must be just,
It should either be all hell or all void.

As people light candles, seeking forgiveness for their sins,
Befriend the wind and extinguish them all,
Those who cannot appreciate their existence should depart from this world as sinners.

Then call upon Adam, from all the stories of the past,
Hold him accountable for what he did to the seven heavens and the seven earths,
Hold him accountable for concealing what he knew and leaving.

Then cling to Moses' cloak and tell him to leave his staff in the Red Sea,
For the sea deemed itself rightful once again, a child of man,
And again man oppressed woman, man, animal, labor, love, and life.
He burned the body, soul, and world with the word of God.

In Cairo

Bury those who deem themselves fragments of God in the pyramid in Cairo,
And write it down in history,
The real culprits are not the pharaohs, but those who do not know how to love.
Have Hammurabi write a decree:
Now all the committed sins will be brought to light face to face,
And those who wounded the ones with love in their hearts will receive the greatest punishment.

Omar Khayyam spoke up:
"Let us raise our glasses now for the crucified loves."
He entered the river flowing with red wine,
Taking a kiss from his beloved, whom he compared to heaven.
With cries of repentance, a revered clergyman passed by,
Thinking the heavens would shatter,
Crying out "Repent, repent!"
And he asked her god, whom she believed in, to rain stones.
But no stones rained from the heavens, and no apocalypse came,
Because of Khayyam, who received a kiss from his beloved.

Noah prays for a storm to save all living beings from the cruelty of humanity,
But it doesn't work;
He still takes all the cruel people on his ark, Noah

He does not hold a grudge against the snake for expelling Adam from paradise,
But every human child who survives
Once again slaughters the delicate beauties of existence.
Neither Noah's prayer
nor the cry of the white dove reaches them.
Even Khidr, who is always ready and present,
Is left powerless in the face of humanity that issues the decree of slaughter.

At Asklepios' Temple

Homer was constructing a temple at Asklepios,
Apollo was descending from Olympus, playing his lyre,
To heal wounded hearts,
He embraced mud, music, sunlight, and the serpent in Pergamon, like a god.
Doctors were engrossed in the task of recreating humanity.
This time, the serpent did not expel humanity from paradise;
It granted healing with the venom it once took lives with,
As if repaying its debt, it poured every drop into glass vials.
Plato takes the floor, the wheel turns, and silence is cut by a sword.
A jury of 501 people demands his last breath with hemlock.
Humanity loves falsehood and does not wish to hear the truth.
That's why they live in fairy tales; they want to be blind to reality.
It's precisely that blindness that takes the lives of all the wise ones,
Because they reveal their darkness,
And fools who mistake their ignorance for truth feel safe in the darkness.
They kill the delicacy of the soul, the reign of love, the charm of words, the rhythm of music.
War feeds them, death feeds them, blood feeds them.
They thirst for human life, and they fill the arenas,
Surrounding the sky with their cries,
As the sands turn red.

Medusa's Gaze

Athena's power is not enough to enchant Poseidon,
Who turned Medusa's head into a monstrous sight
With a curse she bestowed upon the fairest of the fair.
Perseus separates the beautiful head from Medusa's body,
Lybian princess Gorgon Medusa falls victim to an illusion,
From her, Pegasus is born, enchanting the gods with its beauty.

Zeus takes it under his wing, wielding his lightning like feathers.
The gods fall in love with humans,
While the goddesses fill the world with envy and hatred.
The oppressors see the massacres that lead to blasphemy as their right,
Sending every soul they take to Hades.

A war is about to begin.
To some, it's a battle between good and evil.
To others, it's a struggle between the self and the body.
Arjuna lays down his sword and shield, turning to Krishna.
He converses with Him,
First, the Bhagavad Gita emerges, followed by the Mahabharata.

It narrates the struggle, helplessness, and deprivation of humanity,
And foretells that the reign will persist until its death.
Humanity abandons its consciousness, succumbing to the desires of the body,

Killing its brother, its loved ones, and dubs it the battle of good and evil.
Once again, it finds a guise for its cruelty,
Declaring the blood spilled in battle as sacred,
This time, victory is written for the righteous,
and the losers are thrown to the bottom of the caste system,
So that he can cleanse his karma and return in thousands of years.

In the Realm of Dreams

Spirits wandering in the realm of dreams were crafting the world,
At the dawn of the world, Altjira descended to the earth,
He created rivers, streams, seas, mountains, and hills,
He added his own spirit to each one.
Those who embodied were killed beyond the borders of the singing people,
To avoid being seen by humans, he became a rock, water, or a cave on the mountains,
He filled Aboriginal stories and disappeared in the dreamcatcher.
The first human and the sun goddess carrying a torch accompanied him,
And Wagyl, the snake that traveled in dreams, created rivers and streams.

Initially, the world was a chaotic mass with fire and sun,
Rain fell, and the womb of the earth filled with seeds.
First, paradise emerged,
Trees took root,
Flowers bloomed,
Waters flowed,
Lakes grew, seas formed, mountains rose majestically.
Woman painted the earth in vibrant colors.
The god of all times, space, and void, Khaos, invented time in the world.
Seeds sprouted, insects and animals spread across the earth,
They made love with their bodies, souls, and identities,
They multiplied, they multiplied, they multiplied.

Humans emerged somewhere, and humans envied the cycle of nature.
They grew too, multiplied, and multiplied, and multiplied.
That's when hell emerged.
They pierced the heavens with their spears,
Wounded the seas with their arrows,
Killed children with their fiery weapons,
Destroyed cities with their bombs,
Dedicated all their deaths as offerings to the gods they believed in,
Declared the killers heroes,
Declared those who nourished the killers heroes.
They said they did it because the gods wanted it, all the wars.
In wars, the victor was clear,
The loser was both god and humanity.

The Fall of Susanoo

Izanagi gave birth to the sun with a bright drop of water from his left eye,
And the moon god from his right eye,
And from his nose, the trickster god was born.
The arrogant trickster god, Susanoo,
Ruled over the seas and the winds.
One day, he devastated the forests and the mountains,
Killed people, and multiplied their sorrows.
And like Adam, he was banished from the paradise his father, Izanagi, had created.

Those who were expelled from heaven were expelled.
Some ate the apple by obeying the devil and were banished.
Some rebelled in paradise.
Some committed massacres.
Every nation had its own heaven and hell.
Every civilization had its gods and goddesses.
They were divine characters who did not have human silhouettes but behaved like humans.
They did not know love.
They did not know respect.
They did not know virtue.
They made love with their creations.
They multiplied from those of their kind.
They created the world.
In the created world, they passed judgments.
They propagated their lineage.
They took lives.
They demanded sacrifices.
They wanted temples.

Only and only during the dreamtime, they gave dreams,
And promised absolute paradise.

The Search for Love

Humanity was searching for love; the books said that God would provide it.
Humanity was searching for love,
"Abandon yourself, and God will reveal Himself,"
Those who considered themselves saints said so
Humanity was searching for peace,
Those who thought themselves gods invented war and gave weapons to children.

Women wanted justice,
By comparing the man she gave birth to to Susanoo.
Women wanted equality,
By wanting strong men in their lives.
Women wanted heaven,
By accepting that she was created from a man's rib.

The story of man on earth did not end,
Like a spoiled child, it filled the skies in the swallow season.
It migrated in the sad season of autumn,
And the starlings came flocking to replace it.
To frighten their enemies,
Birds painted the sky black

human child,
Looking at those magnificent dances,
was taking pictures
During the dreamtime to experience love.

Mankind was not waking up to its true nature,
Neither was humanity awakening to its humanity,

nor did the gods who created the world take responsibility
and fix the heaven that was turned into hell.
Humanity was searching,
Without knowing what it was searching for.

The Indigenous Child

The Native American child plucked the apple from the branch, asking for permission from the tree,
The apple tree bowed all its branches down in salute to this honorable stance.
The man smiled at the flower,
And thanked the magnificent spirit Wakan-Taka.
All the members of the tribe began to dance with Pow-Wow to multiply happiness and joy,
They blessed their existence as a people who honor death, in the shadow of dream catchers that catch dreams.
Nokomis, who had left her childhood, was sent to befriend a bear to find herself.

The sun and the moon stopped to pray in the sky,
One took the day and the other took the night with its stars.
Man first worshiped them as gods,
Then, when the sky was shrouded in darkness, they offered sacrifices, thinking that it was cursed.
People sacrificed,
They sacrificed animals
In the name of forgiveness for their sins,
They took the lives of beautiful people, saying that I will drive away the evil spirits.

Shaman priest
He took the drum in his hand and went up to the throne,
And with his screams he broke the night,
Those who saw the darkness within themselves in the sky,

Stretched the masters of darkness to the other world on altars,
And to enlighten the ugliness of their souls,
They invented rituals
And shed the blood of tender bodies into sacred bowls.
Leaving the sun and the moon in their place,
Leaving the stars to the night,
Abraham brought Jehovah to the world
To give create to tomorrows without for justice.

During the Harvest Time

At the time of harvest,
He was baptizing his soul in the sin of the wine that touched his lips.
He was rebelling against the stars,
For hiding his dreams behind the clouds.
He was finding his way through the crows,
Who guided him.
Shamans traveled to the Middle World with their drums.
Water lilies blossomed by the lakes,
And the roadsides were adorned with wildflowers.
But he felt sorrow when the storks didn't migrate,
For he couldn't take his body to distant climates.
He called out to the owl nesting in the spruce tree,
Which created a nest for itself.
Colonies of ants surrounded the centipede,
And he was fascinated by the commune life of those whose thoughts didn't match their actions.
The red-tailed fox envied a chicken as its destiny,
Resembling the principle of equal effort and equal sharing.
Someone named Marx and Engels had determined his freedom,
But in the world of those who couldn't satisfy their own desires, hunger and threats were still dominant.
The otters created a dam, and the human who had betrayed his own lake was sacrificing entire civilizations.
The egoistic devil who thought he had his name written in golden letters still walked with confidence,
Without knowing how to satisfy his own ego.

Cats yearning for salvation prepared to face judgment,

Bowing as they looked at themselves in the full-length mirror,
Saluting the door opened by the wolf and the lamb.
A woman walking on cobblestone streets, covering herself with a sheet,
Tried to hide her modesty from those seated on stools.
He missed one sky when he looked at another,
And even the universe, a conglomerate of energy, seemed confused.
The sun wished for the clouds it concealed, and the clouds wished for the sun.
The rain, most of all, lamented its inability to pour its blessings.
Books were scattered on the table,
And pens drew lines under the words.
He couldn't erase those from his life, so they served as reminders.
The mosquito bite on the child's arm resembled the redness of the setting sun behind the hills.
As motorbikes made noise in the streets,
The retired uncles sitting on their balconies held the manhole covers responsible.
They cursed them for making loud noises,
Blaming them for the stench.
This year, the linden tree didn't emit much fragrance, they said,
And the woman shaking her bedsheet by the window was trying to conceal her modesty from shameless onlookers.
He missed one sky when he looked at another,
And even the universe, a conglomerate of energy, seemed confused.
Kittens eager to ascend
Were bowing and saluting Kurt and the lamb.

A woman sitting on a stool was trying to hide her modesty from shameless people.
He missed one sky when he looked at another,
And even the universe, a conglomerate of energy, seemed confused.
Kittens eager to ascend
Were bowing and saluting Kurt and the lamb.
A woman sitting on a stool was trying to hide her modesty from shameless people.
The universe seemed confused, for chaos was its dynamism.
Hunger feeds wisdom, they said,
So they slept for six months, waiting for what would fall into their laps.
By saying that chaos formed the universe, that chaos was an illusion, and illusion was delusion,
He attracted the entire animal kingdom to his side, led by the king of the forests, the mouse.
He exchanged greetings with butterflies each morning,
Feeling a kinship with them.
Travelers of the road, the woman who dries her bedsheet by the window,
Was trying to hide her modesty from those seated on stools.
They discussed whether the beavers had built the dam,
And whether it was the fault of the city that the Anatolian leopard's lineage was on the brink of extinction.
The one with a beard that reached his chest
Was kicking up dust,
While the man who forgot to zip his pants was confidently walking down the street.
Those who spoke of the chaos in the world
Had themselves added to the chaos,

For the busyness of the universe was being ruined by airplanes.
The Siberian wolves' guest
Ordered brown and black syrup with a topknot,
Sipping soda with a thin smile like the moustache on the guards' faces.
The swans were asking to go on the trip of their lives,
Bowing to their full-length mirror.
The door opened to the wolf and the lamb,
And the woman covered herself with a sheet while sitting on a stool.
Looking like she was ashamed, while shameless people
Were walking by.
"Let me say something about love," the rose said, interrupting.
The nightingale's sigh had disappeared, and its sorrow had become words one night.
"I've lost the connection between my emotions and love or love and my emotions,"
It said before ceasing to sing and flying away to a thistle.
Ah, the humans who lamented about these times
Would not have been the victims of melting glaciers or desertifying soil
If they hadn't created existence with their own presence.
Neither the vanishing icebergs nor the desertifying land would have been sacrificed.
The scarlet elk, for the first time, thought, "Existence would not be lost."
He thought of chaos, of the world,
And he felt that the two endpoints of the bridge of Sırat had been described.
Separation from one side was a sharp division,
And from the other side, reunion.
"Meeting is like parting," he thought,

And thousands of gods were created to whom the untimely passersby prayed,
Saying, "Poetry must not be written in vain," Pablo Neruda placed the final period,
And these lines were written by the one who applauded him for his respect.
Claiming rights from the beginning and end of time,
He withdrew quietly to his corner.

Let It Be

"Let every soul be soaked in the rain of its own experience,"
God said.

But Human,
In an attempt to be together from two,
Denied the singularity
...then,
It fell silent.

Time.
It became God.

Of Dreams and Love

Which dream,
Leaves love behind in its wake

Which death,
Does not let yearning live on,
For the departed,
and love for the remaining?

As man forgets to see the dreams of his soul,
He cannot prevent himself from losing himself
In the darkness of his mind.

Hence, for this very reason,
You must teach your soul to dream,
For happiness is the
Is a reflection of the songs your soul sings
In our heart

The Paradox of Self and Other

If I could be in myself,
I couldn't be in you.
It's because I can be you,
That we can be us.

If there's no difference between your "I" and my "I,"
And there's no distinction between your "you" and my "you,"

Then why does departing and longing exist?

On Death and Birth

I pondered upon death,
In the warm, smiling curls of a child's hair.
I contemplated birth,
On the lips of one who came into the world with cries.

Which was real,
To die even though you love?
To be reborn again and again
For the sake of your fragment?

With the knowledge of never being born,
While living through births,
To go toward death in a child's joy...

For the first time, death seemed meaningless
Even though I love it.

We are in the midst of birth...
Knowing we will die...
We were born again

Autumn's Debt

If September owes Autumn,
and is raining
Love drowns the person in tears because it is indebted to separations.
It is not the concern of every darkness to be illuminated
And to seek the light of a candle
Still, in its most generous form,
Autumn gives a rainbow as a gift to September.
And if separations also began to smile
radiated happiness until their jaws were tired,
wanted to find the meaning of life, humans

that's when
what a leaf that falls in the hazan season
neither or will the lover's departure be accounted for...
on the day of reckoning

Contradictions

The contradiction of labor is capital,
The contradiction of love is the beloved,
The contradiction of heaven is the devil,
And the contradiction of my soul is the body.

When all dualities are left behind,
huge
One
nothingness
was staying.

Grain of Sand

For the loves written on a grain of sand,
I would buy the feeling of death from the angels,
In exchange, offering the yearnings for my beloved.

If to meet is the price of death,
I surrender my longing for the beloved
On behalf of those who die every day.

Taking Refuge in Life's End

Having come to the end of life's journey,
I seek refuge in your heart, my beloved,
And I plead for shelter in your soul.

Even though your soul has been invaded by fear,
And even though my plea seems hopeless,
I come again with my dreams on my back,
And I stand at the edge of your smile.

Orange Partings

I harbored orange partings, intruding upon my soul,
Leaving a bitter taste within my mind's hold.
Settling the debts of my sought-after history with fervent fires,
In my eyes, I hold every grain of love's desires.
No matter what anyone might say,
All partings gaze upon humanity through the same window,

And getting accustomed
lasts until the rain ceases,
Until the snow falls,
Until it is spring.

All my partings are now orange,
and I am a traveler,
of my audacious abandonments.

A Village Somewhere

I grew up in geographies whose names I did not even know,
For example, I sought the reality of every dream I saw.
There was a village there, far away, a fragment they taught me by heart when I was a child.
Even if we didn't go, even if we didn't see, that village was our village.

However, to love was not like that,
to go and see,
to see and touch,
and
to touch and smell, it desired.

There is a village there, very far away,
with love sculptures made of marble,
resembling cold winter nights.
There was no remedy in knowing the beauty of the village
until the harvest was reaped from its fields,
until the roots of the saplings were pruned,
and
until its fountain water was tasted.

There is a village there,
suddenly born from a dream of LOVE,
growing in the fear of sweaty nights.

A village where the wind knocks on its door as if it were a breath,
smiling from the dawn of the horizon mornings,

awaiting LOVE like a village,
And
the heart stands for harvest,
like golden wheat ears scattered into the sky as it smiles.

There is a village there,
dedicating its harvest to the beloved,
and praying for love in its supplication.
There is a village
crowded within itself,
a village that is incomplete without MY existence.

Blessed

Now turn
And bless the God within you.
He is
Not in the four religions
Nor in
nor in the words of 128,000 prophets

At Times

Sometimes, death is a departure and a loss,
And at times, death is the greatest of births,
And my friend,
All LOVES
Is born of dead bodies and souls,
Remember.

Addiction to Words

Ours is
a dependence on words
master

Words speak to us
In ways nothing else can.
words don't end
They give us purpose
And they bind us together

Love, Love More

Rejoice...
love more,

and
Choose to be the light of love
in the hell of those with blinded hearts.

The Sparrow and the Hunter

Are you the sparrow, or am I the marksman,
Or could it be the other way around?
Who is struck, who fires the shot,
Why does love get wounded?
Why does the heart hurt when it loves?

They used to say, whichever side the bullet struck the body, it loved from that side,
But love arrives unannounced, strikes without warning, and consumes you,
And
naked is entered into the heart of your lover
beloved
if it darkened your heart
There are no names for these loves, they are loved without reason,
Beloved, if darkness has covered your heart,
fingers holding the sparrow
or
bullets hitting the sparrow
What can she understand from our situation?

The Curtains Fall

One day, the curtains will fall on all stages,
And man will see himself naked.
At that moment, he will understand that
In this life, he is both the actor,
The audience,
And even
The writer of the play.

Since we are the ones on stage,
What are you waiting for?
Turn on the lights.
It is time to be applauded wildly on stage.
It is time to be both audience and actor.
It is time for happiness.

If it is time to be HAPPY,
It is time to tear down all the curtains.

A Poem Borrowed from God

Life was like poetry borrowed from God,
With one hand dipped in water and the other in earth,
God created YOU,
Hence, your hair smells of the ocean, your smile always carries the scent of the earth.

I
Each morning, as stars retreat to their homes,
I gather my share of love from the dough kneaded by God's hands,
I reach for the forbidden tree that will bring you to me,
Plucking love from its branch with my heart prostrating to hell,
I surrender my body to death.

Amidst the devotions made casually,
While seeking exile in your skin through accidental worship,
I search for my SELF,
Inventing fire just like God did on that seventh day of rest,
Seeking my essence.

Ah, just to awaken in you, my love,
I've raised my dreams
To the mornings where the sun rises,
Since that time,
Only in addresses known to angels alone,
I find Myself, lost in you.

The Fault of the Night

All separations were the fault of the night...
Loves pregnant with births that hid their pain in their cries,
Were born in the sexless lovemaking.
Longings were coming into their own,
And newly reborn loves were crying out their duality.
Oh, the un-erect surrenders of my bashful loves,
If you only knew how many times I took the beloved's left breast in my handcuffed palms in a dream.
Still, the breathless states of my lips remained clinging to a foolish passion.
Look, lovers are skipping stars in the night,
Every separation throws their scattered bodies into the arms of another reunion.
That is why
The first one to leave
Is the one who abandons the most
In the unaccepted storms of love.
With a choking cry,
Loves that are indebted to the Book of Death are calling out,
Wake up, they say to the love whose umbilical cord has just been cut,
Wake up and grow,
The one who has hidden its magic in its bleeding tear,
Wake up
And
Grow...

Cold Night

I've stored the warmth of our last embrace
In the sweat droplet on my forehead.
On every cold night I sleep without you,
I will cover myself with it to warm up

The Grave of Death

With the splinter of earth on my fingernail,
I am digging the grave of death.
Humans live their most legitimate journey,
In their most innocent state.
Children's dreams grow by stealing days from death,
Thinking that death will always be lacking no matter how happy we are,
My incomplete drunkenness reaches the bottom of the glasses.

I tell the children, "Don't grow up."
But the children
Leave before me for the colorful world of marbles.

The wind is blowing so suddenly,
The cyclamen flower breaks its neck in my window.
My breath remembers the first death,
The first murder,
The first sacrifice,
The first dedication to self-abandonment.
I take these endless loves from the hand of Cain.

I wanted to surrender
The tears of love from the rose to the nightingale
To the naked rivers in a country house.
Each drop of it
Was borrowed from death
Falling from the lover into my palms.

Mothers cried the most for these unknowing deaths.

And also the Angel of Death, who made a profession of deaths.

Just so mothers don't cry,
I would like to steal eternal life from the gods
And to gift this to all children.

What would be the best?
To bring God down to earth
And ask Him to take all the lives He loves
With his own hand.

For nameless births,
I offer their flowing blood on altars to all the angels,
Naming death "teardrop,"
And I give birth to life
On the night I ignite its fuse with love.

To tell my soul that you also died,
I also surrender it to the fire.
You also died, death,
Die, death,
You,
Death,
Be,

Farewell

Life was like a water droplet, drowning when it hit rock bottom.
Naked and undisturbed, it landed in the midst of desolation like a dewdrop breaking free from its branch, attracting flies to the core of hopelessness.
It was orphaned and alone, like a leaf touched by the wind that had been longing for your breath, leaving it parched.
Advice was given, like the cunning of Ali Baba stealing from the forty thieves' fiery trials.
It became the caliph of kings who laid their cloaks at the doorstep, an ailment called love.
It woke from immense joys without warning, like a mosquito bite, and its pain vanished with the ocean's waves.
My identity would fall into the hand of my mouth, and I would abandon my beloved to a child's tears, stripped of love and nakedness.

Farewell, to the timid passion of my beginning,
Farewell, to the word "I love you" lodged in my throat,
Farewell, the innocent lie of my sudden departure,
Farewell, when I forget the scent of your sweat on my pillow upon awakening,
Farewell.

In Exile in a Dragonfly's Wing

In a love, akin to exile on a dragonfly's wing, humanity resided...
Building a nest upon a droplet,
Growing by dusting a leaf with its presence, incessantly.

That is why,
In lost examinations,
It lived by depleting earned lifetimes
In pursuit of love, disappearing

The Loss of Syllables

At times, I contemplate
I think I have lost my syllables.
Neither in my left pocket are the words,
Nor in my right pocket,

I find my words absent,
Caught in a peculiar wave,
The waves sway me in their palms,

My mind becomes a jumble,
I fall into a syllable.
I light a light,
It dances on the water,

I christen it with a name,
Name, Sea-foam,
Sharing its loneliness with myself.

There remains just me,
And a small drop on my skin,
Its existence is a remnant of the ocean
I name it tear,
By rubbing it on my cheeks,
I flow gently
From myself
To myself

I Have Always Been Fifty

I was always fifty years old.
For every birth I've held in my palm,
I've gathered an equal share of death in my satchel.
I bent my heart in the courts where women sought justice,
Sometimes, I ascended to the heavens, speaking to the mute sky,
Other times, I descended seven layers below, scorching my rebellious body with fire.

I was alone in the places where tales of solitude were recited,
I cast my ancestors as the seven-headed dragon before me,
Each head carrying its own troubles and remedies, mirroring my seven-layered self.
Death was red, and it took on a material form in my soul,
Orange bore a sense of guilt, a helpless feeling within existence's birth,

Yellow embraced the shadows, defying the sun, and all my pains lay within it.
Then came green, yearning for love, and it remained the fourth head in my heart,
Blue would speak out, saying, "One day, you'll understand everything I've shown you. You'll burn not with your fears, but with the color you couldn't perceive."
And the seventh, the one draped in purple, would burst forth in ecstasy, breaking free from the captivity of your awakened heart, urging you to break the bonds of both fire and wind.
As I said, it was the tale itself that was my existence,
Building heaven on top of the seven layers,

Constructing hell beneath them,
Hiding my soul in the depths of my mind,
Summoning me beyond the mountains of Kaf with the sleeping beauty's tale.

My age is always fifty, I am within the last moments of my life now,
My age is always fifty,
Always fifty...

Love says

Love says,
What's within you will come to you,
And life will show what you'll receive in return for what you give.

My darling,
that beginning will my lips' loves conceive if I die on the way,
If I release my soul to the garden of sorrow without seeing it?
If I die on the road, what kind of beginning will my lips and kisses conceive?

The water droplet had taught me to touch with the tips of my fingers
Every arrival should have carried itself beyond the pages of history it had shouldered.
It should not have asked why.
And there should be no "I wish."
It should not have waited for tomorrow.
Nor should it have come out of yesterday.
Love should have only existed in the present and in you.

That's when
The body surrenders itself to a big hug,
Life, beautifies with the justice of existence,
I borrow a happy smile from your friendship
My being is grateful as I share
Abandons itself to a big hug,
And the hidden "me" within it
Becomes Love and falls into timelessness.
in your arms

Our hearts fell to a wild love

We were coming from beyond the bounds of time,
Naked to ourselves, dressed against the world.
Our hearts ached, our vernacular defied description.
Our souls fell recklessly into a fervent love,
As if we had committed theft, we concealed the beloved we gazed upon with love...
We drew fragrances from the soil,
We daubed impromptu joys upon ourselves.
We were children without identities,
We were walking around with snot in our noses and snot marks on our arms

In the streets where God's voice echoed from the minarets, we knelt,
The imam of the neighborhood would read the call to prayer of growing up that was binding.
We would search for the heroes of our creation story on the ever-lengthening roads.
We would look at time, be silent to ourselves, and talk to books and notebooks
with our eyes separated from the drops.

We grew up
We broke up
We were no longer the child who was born
Nor the child in the process of growing.

Every moment, in a different yearning,
We experienced back-and-forths between the warmth of the mother's womb and the weight of the earth that would cover us.

Because birth may take a life from a human,
We surrender all stories to calendar numbers and march into the future.
Now,
Today is made of yesterday, and tomorrow is composed of moments,
We wake up in the morning and scatter in the field
To multiply new flowers.
Welcome to life,
Welcome child to life,

The last drop of water falling from the fern called us.
We took scents from the soils
In the love of spreading beautiful fragrances.

I Grew Up with Wishes

I grew up with wishes in my pocket,
Of a magic wand that would make all things right.

I listened to children pray for a better world,
And I witnessed the prayers of the poor asking for money from the sky

I saw parents
with their dying children in their arms
I witnessed parents grieving for children they lost,
In their arms, the heaviest of burdens they'd bear,
And my own prayers could not put out their fire.

Since God broke my magic wand,
took power into his own hands,
Since then, humanity's woes, I watched dismayed,
As suffering and oppression filled the space.
And I, amidst sorrows, continued to fade away,

Humanity and children have known only pain and death.

And I,
In agonys,
I keep dying

The Sound of Absence

In moments when subjects vanished, predicates astray,
The rainbird's song, in my ears did sway,
The longing found in Kafka's letters to Milena,
Nazım's verses for Vera, Dante's for Beatrice's arena,
Echoed in my heart, meter amiss, led astray.

The poet proclaimed, "In poetry's embrace,
Lie devoted vows to love's sacred grace,
Love's is kept in its own dream."
and
In the verses, Jesus says, "Love clothes your overdue
dreams on our souls as new,"
Thus, poems grew weary,
At the core of poetry, where inspiration flows.

Every morning, I wake to the new ache
Of longing for the beloved
I feel her breath on my neck
As I watched the birds' wings take flight towards their
tryst,
Like I'm on the sweet abyss of love.

As I wipe the drops of water that multiply in my palm
With my fingertips,
I draw my dreams
On the trunk of the sequoia tree,
Monsoon rains take me from the lap of the oceans in
cascades,
and me
I hang my dreams on the branches of the redwoods

When I discovered letters that contained your grace,

In your eyes, I found joy's warm embrace,
Like a babe tasting a mother's embrace,
Your eyes encompass my life's entire space,
And every time I look at them,
I'm getting drunk
You flow like red wine distilled from grapes
and
That intoxicates my soul, all time

In the F sharp note of Rodrigo's guitar concerto playing on the radio,
I catch the last moment of time spent without you.

A new music begins,
My eyelashes, bass baritone loves you with screams,
In my ears, blues' melodies that never depart,

The rhythm of country music in my throat, my absence in the vortex of my heart
And starlings taking refuge in every letter of "I love you"
Making my soul dance, in this love

The Poem of Beginnings

"Can you write poetry, Child?" God asked, and the Child replied...
In the midst of winter, LOVE...
I was a Syrian passion,
Brought to life by my fragile, hope-bearing mother,
Accumulating the rebellions that shattered my father's harvest.
With only two dirhams and a kernel of life,
I was wandering through the winter-sung songs.

I was the beneficiary of faith, inheriting it from Jesus,
I was the guardian of souls, watching over them from the Red Sea.
While I was trading in the winter, I was giving away the strings of my saz
To a verse, a word, a line, I gave Mecnun's lost love its pain.
Jesus spoke through the crucifixion, giving life from his own life,
He released his bandits to Anatolia, interceding through love.
He filled Yunus's belly with the bitter fires of wine,
Nimrod held the tip of the flame,
And Ibrahim secluded himself, with wood turned into fish by the love of God.

The Peacock Angel declared, "The truth lies in knowing that man is man,"
Yet man was searching outside for the knowledge that holds the secret.

The cry of the wounded külüng pierced Shirin's heart in the hands of Amasya,
Aslı ignited her hair, merging with Kerem's ashes,
To the wings of the Phoenix...

Hünkâr breathes life into Yunus's fire,
Yet Yunus's ignorance receives grains of wheat as its portion.
Yunus was devoted to love for forty years in Tapduk's dergah,
And the cedar tree shatters the patience of its slender, long branches.

The hoopoe bird asks,
Who turns inward to reach the essence?
Who wields Shams's pen and throws Celalettin into hell?

And in the night's embrace, a song blooms in the heart,
Which verse, which chapter, which prayer can heal a heart that has lost its tongue?
God sets the world on fire,
Man, deaf to himself, blind to love, mute to life, dies in the midst of all loves.
Cities burn,
Children's smiles fade away,
Drunken men who overturn wine bottles can't find their mothers,
All creatures descend from heaven,
And they hand over their rewards to hell in exile for their beloveds.

Hell extinguishes itself for the sake of love,
The one who kindles the fire feels ashamed,
Those who carry wood to the fire feel ashamed,

The needle's tip, which chains the sinner in time, feels ashamed,
Heaven smiles upon those who leave.

They hope for salvation, surrendering their heads to Ibrahim's knife,
Pharaoh collects the wealth of the people of faith,
And angels collect tears from David's fiery house.
No matter how many days Davut fasts, he doesn't return, having died for love.

Job's wound fills with the seven degrees of faith,
Books fall silent, people speak, sins multiply,
Forty birds fly to the Kaf Mountain to receive gifts from their kings.
Oh, mountain, says the bird with the burnt wing,
The one who comes is you, it is when you come,
The one who is created is you, and the creator is also you,
The one who ignites is you, and the one who is ignited is you,
The one who knows is you, and the one who seeks to know is also you,
The one who sees is you, and the one who desires to see is also you,
In the lover, it's you, and in love, it's you,
In the book, it's you, and in the one who writes, it's also you.

The Simurgh becomes a reality in the last days,
The doors of Araf burn,
There is neither heaven left behind nor hell,
Time is lost,
Supposition is lost,
Moment is lost,

And it emerges... (period)
It becomes the beginning,
It becomes the end,
It becomes a Syrian abandonment in Alexandria,
Zeus becomes Olympus,
Odin's Valaskialf in Asgard becomes life.

Ravens carry messages
From dreams to reality,
Plato drinks poison for the sake of his beliefs,
Aristotle shouts for justice,
Nietzsche says it this way,
And Freud writes about humanity like a child who finds pleasure in his mother.
At the highest cathedral, Quasimodo cries out atop Notre Dame's hunchback,
She is silent, the black mare in the Sahara.

And
Picasso paints the first pang of the final death in Guernica in black and white,
A German officer asks, "Did you create this painting?" and Picasso responds, "No, you did."
As with every death, humanity multiplies every war within itself.
Fathers and Sons are dying,
Mothers are left behind,
The scent of their skin is sold as war booty,
And the one who takes life captures the scent the most.

Heaven sulks,
Hell remains silent,
God watches,
And

Life continues,
People also say so,
To live...
To live
Live
Love
And then, in all unknown stories,
A lament,
A silence,
A Saint carrying the temple on his shoulders,
Drawing the bridge of the universe on the artery of existence with his staff,
He lets go
of his soul.

Rediscovering Poetry

Within me there is a strange and unfathomable poem,
But words do not turn to verse...
Or verse cannot become words.
It is as if I have lost the stories that would define this vast and deep void.
I wander over the keys like a child who has just begun to speak,
But his vocabulary is not yet fully stocked.
I am fighting a covert battle with myself,
For if I confess, my soul will be imprisoned by my mind.
If I remain silent, my heart will burst from the noise of my mind.

I say "poem,"
But it is not written by sitting down.
It requires a lover,
Wine,
Longing,
And love.
I do not remember where I took this man from,
Nor can I count how many poems I wrote without love or affection.

Now,
As my body sways back and forth in the arms of the night,
I will catch the syllables and make words from them,
And then I will pour the words into lines.

How can a person be so alien to his own heart?
At what age does he abandon his laughter?

Does he leave the sun without a morning?
Does he apologize to the dried-up geraniums he neglected and killed?
Does he spend his life with false accusations?
Does the poet write the poem for the lover,
Or does the lover become the poem and write herself?
I do not know.

So it is,
My poem
Is composed of lines that have lost their emotion,
And
I said to you, "I will complain to you," in the style of a poem,
All by myself.
The poem
Has left me
And I have lost the poem
On this night.
Perhaps it will hear my plea
And
A few words will cling to my side.
They will speak of this and that,
And then they will bring up poetry and love.

Perhaps
I will remember
How to write a poem from a single note,
And how to become love from a single word.

www.ingramcontent.com/pod-product-compliance
Lightning Source LLC
LaVergne TN
LVHW050323160826
845677LV00014B/3517
9798882161681